★ *Voices from the Civil War* ★

CONFEDERATE GENERALS

edited by Tom Head

BLACKBIRCH®
PRESS

THOMSON
★
™
GALE

San Diego • Detroit • New York • San Francisco • Cleveland
New Haven, Conn. • Waterville, Maine • London • Munich

THOMSON

★

™

GALE

For more information, contact
The Gale Group, Inc.
27500 Drake Rd.
Farmington Hills, MI 48331-3535
Or you can visit our Internet site at http://www.gale.com

Photo credits: Cover, pages 7, 14, 15, 19, 21 © CORBIS; pages 5, 17, 29 © Hulton Archive; pages 8 (Davis), 9 (Lincoln) © Digital Stock; pages 8, 9, 12, 13, 18, 23, 26, 27 © Library of Congress; page 16 © Blackbirch Archive; page 30 © Snark / Art Resource, NY

LIBRARY OF CONGRESS CATALOGING-IN-PUBLICATION DATA

Head, Tom.
  Confederate generals / [compiled by] Tom Head.
    p. cm. — (Voices from the Civil War)
  Includes bibliographical references (p. 31) and index.
   ISBN 1-56711-790-2 (hardback : alk. paper)
  1. Generals—Confederate States of America—Biography. 2. Confederate States of America. Army—Biography. 3. United States—History—Civil War, 1861–1865—Personal narratives, Confederate. I. Head, Tom II. Series.

E467.C77 2003
 973.7'3'0922—dc21

                                 2002027797

Printed in United States
10 9 8 7 6 5 4 3 2 1

Contents

LEADING A REBELLION

When the Civil War broke out in April 1861, the Confederacy was financially weak and its military was untested in battle. Early Southern leaders had no way of knowing how many Union generals might join the South, or how many soldiers they might be able to assemble into an army. They also did not know if they would be able to train and equip those soldiers for battle.

In contrast, the Union had a large and well-equipped army that had experience fighting in three consecutive wars. At the very beginning of the Civil War, all of the greatest military leaders of the Mexican-American War held a Union commission. The popular belief was that the Union would be able to swiftly destroy the Confederacy and reunite the nation.

The Confederacy was lucky that some of the greatest Union military minds, including General Robert E. Lee (considered by many at the time to be the most brilliant American military leader alive), left their federal posts and joined the Confederacy. Their reasons for doing so, though, were as varied as their personalities.

For Lee, it was the love of his home state of Virginia. Although he condemned the South's practice of slavery as a "moral and political evil," he could not fight against his fellow Virginians. When Virginia seceded—or left the Union—and U.S. president Abraham Lincoln ordered all U.S. generals to crush the Confederate rebellion, Lee resigned his U.S. commission and joined the Confederacy.

Others, such as millionaire slave trader Nathan Bedford Forrest, had less difficulty choosing which side to take. Forrest was unable to secure an immediate command, so he decided to pay for and equip his own cavalry unit. He then donated the unit to the Confederacy—on the condition that he would be its leader. He quickly proved that he had a natural gift for military strategy.

Most Confederate generals were neither as torn as Lee nor as confident as Forrest. Many generals were products of the South's privileged upper class. Experienced generals such as Joseph E. Johnston and P.G.T. Beauregard felt

Confederate general Robert E. Lee (on horse, right), here shown meeting with another rebel general, "Stonewall" Jackson (on horse, left), was believed by some to be the most brilliant military leader in America.

obligated to defend the Southern way of life against the North, which they saw as an invading force. Southern traditions had defined the way their families had lived for centuries, and the generals did not want to see that taken away from them. President Lincoln had been elected with only 40 percent of the popular vote, and with almost no Southern support.

In taking a stand, the Confederacy never intended to conquer the North. Instead, Southerners hoped to create a new country called the Confederate States of America. On the other hand, the goal of the Union was to preserve the United States as a single nation. Most of the battles of the Civil War took place in Southern states, which contributed to the Confederates' view that they were being invaded. It also gave the Confederacy a strategic advantage. Because the South was fighting a defensive war, they did not have to win decisively. All they hoped to do was prolong the war until the North tired of fighting and let the Southerners have their own nation.

The war, however, did not turn out that way. By the later years of fighting, the Union had more than twice as many soldiers as the Confederacy (2.5 million Union troops versus 1 million Confederate troops), and those soldiers were far better equipped. This was because of the Union's stronger economy. The determined Confederate army, led by generals considered to be some of the most skilled in the nation's history, managed to hold off a Union victory for four years. The

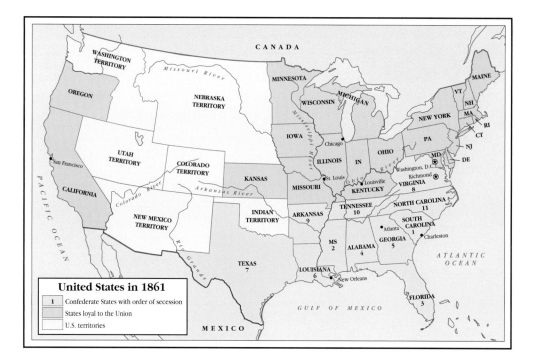

Rows upon rows of headstones mark the graves of fallen Confederate soldiers. An estimated 258,000 rebel soldiers died in the Civil War.

South paid a terrible price: An estimated 258,000 Confederate soldiers died in the war, including beloved generals such as "Stonewall" Jackson and J.E.B. Stuart.

When Confederate general Robert E. Lee surrendered in April 1865, the Civil War ended. Many generals accepted this and lived peacefully within the Union, but others resented the Union government and challenged it in other ways. Nathan Bedford Forrest played a role in creating the Ku Klux Klan, a violent racist group that would not accept blacks as equal citizens after the war. Jubal Early fled to Mexico to start up a new Confederate States of America there (though he quickly changed his mind due to lack of support). For his part, Robert E. Lee accepted defeat and encouraged other Southerners to do the same. Many Confederate generals who became law-abiding Union citizens, nevertheless, remained committed to the idea that the South would one day become an independent nation.

★ Chronology of the Civil War ★

November 1860

Abraham Lincoln is elected president of the United States.

December 1860–March 1861

- Concerned about Lincoln's policy against slavery in the West, the South Carolina legislature unanimously votes to secede from the United States. Alabama, Florida, Georgia, Louisiana, Mississippi, and Texas secede from the Union, and form the Confederate States of America.

- Mississippi senator Jefferson Davis becomes president of the Confederacy.

- Arkansas, North Carolina, Tennessee, and Virginia later join the rebellion.

April 1861

Confederate troops fire on Union-occupied Fort Sumter in South Carolina and force a surrender. This hostile act begins the Civil War.

September 1862–January 1863

- Lee's Army of Northern Virginia and George McClellan's Army of the Potomac fight the war's bloodiest one-day battle at Antietam, Maryland. Though the battle is a draw, Lee's forces retreat to Virginia.

- Abraham Lincoln issues the Emancipation Proclamation that declares all slaves in Confederate states to be forever free. Three months later it takes effect.

September 1864

Atlanta, Georgia, surrenders to Union general William T. Sherman, who orders Atlanta evacuated and then burned. Over the coming months, he begins his March to the Sea to Savannah. His troops destroy an estimated $100 million worth of civilian property in an attempt to cut rebel supply lines and reduce morale.

Jefferson Davis, president of the Confederate States of America

July 1861

Confederate troops defeat Union forces at the First Battle of Manassas (First Bull Run) in Fairfax County, Virginia, the first large-scale battle of the war.

April 1862

• Confederate troops are defeated at the Battle of Shiloh in Tennessee. An estimated 23,750 soldiers are killed, wounded, or missing, more than in all previous American wars combined.

• Slavery is officially abolished in the District of Columbia; the only Union slave states left are Delaware, Kentucky, Maryland, and Missouri.

June 1862

General Robert E. Lee assumes command of the Conferate Army of Northern Virginia.

Robert E. Lee

August 1862

Confederate troops defeat Union forces at the Second Battle of Manassas (Second Bull Run) in Prince William County, Virginia.

July 1863

Union forces stop the South's invasion of the North at Gettysburg, Pennsylvania. Lasting three days, it is the bloodiest battle of the war.

November 1863

President Abraham Lincoln delivers the Gettysburg Address in honor of those who died at the war's bloodiest battle at Gettysburg.

April 1865

• Confederate general Robert E. Lee surrenders to Union general Ulysses S. Grant. This ends the Civil War on April 9.

• Five days later, President Lincoln is assassinated by actor John Wilkes Booth.

December 1865

The Thirteenth Amendment becomes law and abolishes slavery in the United States.

Abraham Lincoln, president of the United States of America

★ P.G.T. Beauregard ★
REQUESTING THE SURRENDER OF FORT SUMTER

P.G.T. Beauregard was appointed superintendent of West Point Military Academy in January 1861. When he was ordered to help prepare the Union army for civil war, Beauregard—unwilling to go to war with his own home state of Louisiana—resigned his commission and joined the Confederacy. Confederate leaders quickly began to take command of federal military bases in their home states. The only holdout was Fort Sumter in South Carolina, which was commanded by Major Robert Anderson. In this letter to Anderson, Beauregard requests that he surrender the fort. Anderson initially refused, but gave in after several days of Confederate bombardment. Although Beauregard avoided bloodshed, the Battle of Fort Sumter was the first military conflict of the Civil War.

- **P.G.T. Beauregard, First Letter to Maj. Robert Anderson (April 11, 1861), in *The War of the Rebellion*, series I, 53 volumes. Washington: Government Printing Office, 1880–1901.**

Sir: The Government of the Confederate States has hitherto forborne from any hostile demonstration against Fort Sumter, in the hope that the Government of the United States, with a view to the amicable adjustment of all questions between the two Governments, and to avert the calamities of war, would voluntarily evacuate it.

There was reason at one time to believe that such would be the course pursued by the Government of the United States, and under that impression my Government has refrained from making any demand for the surrender of the fort. But the Confederate States can no longer delay assuming actual possession of a fortification commanding the entrance of one of their harbors, and necessary to its defense and security.

I am ordered by the Government of the Confederate States to demand the evacuation of Fort Sumter. My aides, Colonel Chesnut and Captain Lee, are authorized to make such demand of you. All proper facilities will be afforded for the removal of yourself and command, together with company arms and property, and all private property, to any post in the United States which you may select. The flag which you have upheld so long and with so much fortitude, under the most trying circumstances, may be saluted by you on taking it down.

Colonel Chesnut and Captain Lee will, for a reasonable time, await your answer.

GLOSSARY
- **hitherto:** until now
- **forborne:** refrained
- **amicable:** friendly
- **avert:** avoid
- **fortitude:** strength
- **calamities:** disasters

★ *Albert Sidney Johnston* ★
TRYING TO SAVE FORT DONELSON

A native of Kentucky, Albert Sidney Johnston became a U.S. Army lieutenant in 1827. By the time the Civil War broke out in 1861, Johnston had become a general, and was regarded as one of the finest military minds in the country. With a Confederate army, Johnston took control of Bowling Green, Kentucky, in January 1862. Johnston withdrew from his home state, however, to reinforce Confederate forces in Mississippi and Tennessee. In this excerpt from a letter to Confederacy president Jefferson Davis, Johnston explains his risky decision to withdraw from Bowling Green and relocate his army.

- **Albert Sidney Johnston, Letter to President Jefferson Davis, March 18, 1862.**

T he evacuation of Bowling Green was imperatively necessary, and was ordered before, and executed while the battle was being fought at [Fort] Donelson. I had made every disposition for the defence of the fort my means allowed; and the troops were among the best of my force. The Generals . . . were high in the opinion of officers and men for skill and courage, and among the best officers of my command. They were popular with the volunteers, and all had seen much service. No reinforcements were asked. I awaited the event opposite Nashville. The result of the conflict each day was favorable. At midnight on the 15th, I received news of a glorious victory—at dawn, of a defeat. . . .

Nashville was incapable of defence from its position, and from the forces advancing from Bowling Green and up the Cumberland. A rear guard was left under General Floyd to secure the stores and provisions, but did not completely effect the object. The people were horrified, and some of the troops were disheartened. The discouragement was spreading, and I ordered the command to Murfreesboro', where I managed . . . to collect an army able to offer battle. The weather was inclement, the floods excessive, and the bridges were washed away, but most of the stores and provisions were saved, and conveyed to new depots. This having been accomplished, though with serious loss, in conformity with my original design, I marched Southward and crossed the Tennessee [River] at this point, so as to co-operate or unite with General [P.G.T.] Beauregard, for the defence of the Valley of the Mississippi. The passage is almost completed, and the head of my column is already with General [Braxton] Bragg at Corinth. The movement was deemed too hazardous by the most experienced members of my staff, but the object warranted the risk.

GLOSSARY
- **imperatively:** urgently
- **disposition:** effort
- **inclement:** poor
- **conveyed:** transported

★ Joseph E. Johnston ★
VICTORY AT MANASSAS

On July 21, 1861, Union troops attacked a vastly outnumbered Confederate force in Manassas, Virginia. To most Union military advisors, the logic was clear: a few large-scale victories would show Confederate leaders that their armies could not maintain a rebellion for long. At first, things seemed to go as planned. Union troops managed to weaken the Confederate line of defense and were able to advance. Then Confederate reinforcements arrived. Suddenly, the Union troops were slightly outnumbered and facing a counterattack from an army of unknown size. They were forced to retreat, and the Union lost the first large-scale battle of the Civil War. Leading the counterattack was General Joseph E. Johnston, a veteran of the Mexican-American War who joined the Confederacy when his home state of Virginia seceded in April 1861. In the following report on the battle, Johnston commends his troops for standing their ground.

- **Joseph E. Johnston, Report on the Battle of Manassas (October 14, 1861), in *The War of the Rebellion*, series I, 53 volumes. Washington: Government Printing Office, 1880–1901.**

Our victory was as complete as one gained by infantry and artillery can be. An adequate force of cavalry would have made it decisive. It is due, under Almighty God, to the skill and resolution of General Beauregard, the admirable conduct of Generals Bee, E.K. Smith, and Jackson, and of Colonels (commanding brigades) Evans, Cocke, Early, and Elzey, and the courage and unyielding firmness of our patriotic volunteers. The admirable character of our troops is incontestably proved by the result of this battle, especially when it is remembered that little more than

Gen. Joseph E. Johnston led the counterattack at the Battle of Manassas.

This painting depicts the fighting at the Battle of Manassas, Virginia, in July 1861. The Confederacy won this first major battle of the Civil War.

six thousand men of the Army of the Shenandoah with sixteen guns [cannons], and less than two thousand of that of the Potomac with six guns, for full five hours successfully resisted thirty-five thousand U.S. troops with a powerful artillery and a superior force of regular cavalry. Our forces engaged, gradually increasing during the remainder of the contest, amounted to but blank men at the close of the battle. The brunt of this hard-fought engagement fell upon the troops who held their ground so long with such heroic resolution. The unfading honor which they won was dearly bought with the blood of many of our best and bravest. Their loss was far heavier in proportion than that of the troops coming later into action. . . .

Twenty-eight pieces of artillery, about five thousand muskets, and nearly five hundred thousand cartridges, a garrison flag, and ten colors were captured on the field or in the pursuit. Besides these we captured sixty-four artillery horses, with their harness, twenty-six wagons, and much camp equipage, clothing, and other property abandoned in their flight.

The officers of my staff deserve high commendation for their efficient and gallant services during the day and the campaign, and I beg leave to call the attention of the Government to their merits.

> **GLOSSARY**
> - **unyielding:** unbending
> - **incontestably:** without question
> - **Potomac:** a small Confederate army based in Virginia; not the Union's massive Army of the Potomac, which was formed shortly after the Battle of Manassas.
> - **colors:** regimental flags
> - **equipage:** equipment

★ *Braxton Bragg* ★

WHY WE LOST AT SHILOH

In July 1861, both Union and Confederate leaders were stunned by the Battle of Manassas. It was the first major land battle of the war and it ended with a thundering Confederate victory. The battle began well for the Union, but the Confederacy drove the federal army back and established that the war would not be easily won. In April 1862, both sides received a somber surprise at the Battle of Shiloh. Things went well for the Confederacy on the first day of fighting as Confederate general Braxton Bragg led his regiments to what appeared to be a Confederate victory. When Union reinforcements arrived on the second day, the tide turned and the Confederates retreated. The battle was very costly. Twenty-four thousand soldiers were dead, wounded, or missing. The casualties were higher than in all previous American wars combined. In this excerpt from his April 30 report on the battle, Bragg reflects on the factors that led to a Confederate defeat at Shiloh.

- **Braxton Bragg, Report on the Battle of Shiloh (April 30, 1862), in** *The War of the Rebellion,* **series I, 53 volumes. Washington: Government Printing Office, 1880–1901.**

I t may not be amiss to refer briefly to the causes it is believed operated to prevent the complete overthrow of the enemy, which we were so near accomplishing, and which would have changed the entire complexion of the war. The want of proper organization and discipline, and the inferiority in many cases of our officers to the men they were expected to command, left us often without system or order. . . . Especially was this the case after the occupancy of each of the enemy's camps, the spoils of which served to delay and greatly to demoralize our men. But no one cause probably contributed so largely to our loss of time—which was the loss of success—as the fall of the commanding general [Joseph E. Johnston, who had been wounded in battle]. At the moment of this irreparable disaster the plan of battle was being rapidly and successfully executed under his immediate eye and lead on the right.

For want of a common superior to the different commands on that part of the field great delay

Gen. Braxton Bragg was the Confederate leader at the Battle of Shiloh.

Union forces face off against the Confederates in this print depicting the Battle of Shiloh at Pittsburg Landing, Tennessee, in 1862. It was the bloodiest battle in U.S. history up to that time.

occurred after this misfortune, and that delay prevented the consummation of the work so gallantly and successfully begun and carried on until the approach of night induced our new commander to recall the exhausted troops for rest and recuperation before a crowning effort on the next morning.

The arrival during the night of a large and fresh army to re-enforce the enemy, equal in numbers at least to our own, frustrated all his well-grounded expectations, and, after a long and bloody contest with superior forces, compelled us to retire from the field, leaving our killed, many of our wounded, and nearly all of the trophies of the previous day's victories.

In this result we have a valuable lesson, by which we should profit—never on a battle-field to lose a moment's time, but leaving the killed, wounded, and spoils to those whose special business it is to care for them, to press on with every available man, giving a panic-stricken and retreating foe no time to rally, and reaping all the benefits of a success never complete until every enemy is killed, wounded, or captured.

> **GLOSSARY**
> - **amiss:** wrong
> - **overthrow:** defeat
> - **demoralize:** reduce the fighting spirit
> - **irreparable:** unfixable
> - **consummation:** completion

★ *Ambrose Powell Hill* ★

ON THE DEFENSIVE IN VIRGINIA

A veteran of the Mexican-American War, Ambrose Powell Hill resigned his federal commission when his home state of Virginia seceded from the Union in April 1861. He became a general in the Confederacy in February 1862. In early August 1862, the Confederate Army was fending off attacks from Union forces in Virginia. At the Battle of Cedar Mountain, Confederate troops faced an attack from Union forces and a likely defeat. A well-timed counterattack from Hill—described here in an excerpt from his battle report—drove the Union attackers back. Several weeks later, the Union defeat at the Battle of Second Manassas drove off the Union assault on Virginia. On April 2, 1865, less than a week before the Confederacy surrendered, Hill rode off to meet his army and was intercepted by Union scouts who shot and killed him.

Ambrose Powell Hill

• **A.P. Hill, Report on the Battle of Cedar Mountain, in *The War of the Rebellion*, series I, 53 volumes. Washington: Government Printing Office, 1880–1901.**

B etween 4 and 5 o'clock—the wagons of [Confederate General Richard] Ewell still passing and a portion of [Thomas "Stonewall"] Jackson's division still not having crossed the river—I received an order from General Jackson to go back to Orange Court-House and encamp for the night. The head of my column having only made about a mile, I bivouacked the brigades where they were.

That night I sent a note to General Jackson . . . that it would be impossible for me to get along the next day with my artillery unless the road was cleared of the trains; that, familiar with the country, if he would permit, I could take my division by a short road by the ford at Holliday's Mill and join him at any point he might designate. The reply I received was that the trains had been ordered from the road, and to move immediately by the route first designated, as it was his intention to be in Culpeper Court-House that night. . . . Arriving within about 6 miles of Culpeper Court-House, the heavy firing in front gave notice that the battle had commenced. I was directed by General Jackson to send a brigade to the support of [General William] Taliaferro, who

This print shows Union troops charging the Confederate front at the Battle of Cedar Mountain, Virginia. A well-timed Confederate counterattack drove off the Union forces and won the day for the South.

was in line of battle on the right of the main road. . . . Without waiting for the formation of the entire line [General Lawrence] Branch was immediately ordered forward, and passing through the broken brigade received the enemy's fire, promptly returned it, checked the pursuit, and in turn drove them back and relieved Taliaferro's flank. The enemy, driven across an open field, had rallied in a wood skirting it. . . . The enemy were charged across this field. . . . General [Edward Lloyd] Thomas, on the right, had been ordered by General Jackson to the right. . . . Thomas formed his line of battle along a fence bordering a corn field, through which the enemy were advancing. After a short contest here the enemy were hurled back.

★ Thomas J. "Stonewall" Jackson ★

"STONEWALL" JACKSON ATTACKS

August 1862 brought the Battle of Second Manassas and new hope for the Confederate cause. After months of military defeats, the Confederate army claimed a major victory and established that the war was not yet over. During the first day of fighting on August 28, Confederate forces were led by Thomas J. Jackson. A hero of the first Battle of Manassas, Jackson was known for his courage and intense military discipline. His troops were among the most successful and aggressive in the entire Confederate army. Jackson's brilliant grasp of military strategy impressed both his troops and his enemies. In this excerpt from his report on the Battle of Second Manassas, Jackson describes the first day of fighting and commends his Union opponents for their "obstinate determination."

- **Thomas Jonathan Jackson, Report on the Battle of Second Manassas, in *The War of the Rebellion*, series I, 53 volumes. Washington: Government Printing Office, 1880–1901.**

My command had hardly concentrated north of the turnpike before the enemy's advance reached the vicinity of Groveton from the direction of Warrenton. General [J.E.B.] Stuart and his cavalry kept me advised of the general movements of the enemy. . . . Dispositions were promptly made to attack the enemy, based upon the idea that he would continue to press forward upon the turnpike toward Alexandria; but as he did not appear to advance in force, and there was reason to believe that his main body was leaving the road and inclining toward Manassas Junction, my command was advanced through the woods, leaving Groveton on the left, until it reached a commanding position. . . . By this time

"Stonewall" Jackson

Union forces (foreground) gather to meet the attack of "Stonewall" Jackson's Confederate troops (background) in the Battle of Second Manassas in 1862. It was a decisive but short-lived Southern victory.

it was sunset; but as his [the enemy's] column appeared to be moving by, with its flank exposed, I determined to attack at once. . . . The batteries . . . were placed in position . . . above the village of Groveton, and, firing over the heads of our skirmishers, poured a heavy fire of shot and shell upon the enemy. This was responded to by a very heavy fire from the enemy, forcing our batteries to select another position. By this time [General William] Taliaferro's command . . . was advanced from the woods to the open field, and was now moving in gallant style until it reached an orchard on the right of our line and was less than 100 yards from a large force of the enemy. The conflict here was fierce and sanguinary. Although largely reenforced, the Federals did not attempt to advance, but maintained their ground with obstinate determination.

Both lines stood exposed to the discharges of musketry and artillery until about 9 o'clock, when the enemy slowly fell back, yielding the field to our troops.

Although the enemy moved off under cover of the night and left us in quiet possession of the field, he did not long permit us to remain inactive or in doubt as to his intention to renew the conflict.

> **GLOSSARY**
> - **vicinity:** area
> - **dispositions:** arrangements
> - **inclining:** heading
> - **batteries:** artillery regiments
> - **skirmishers:** scouts
> - **sanguinary:** bloody
> - **reenforced:** reinforced
> - **obstinate:** stubborn
> - **discharges:** firing
> - **yielding:** leaving

★ James Ewell Brown Stuart ★

THE LAST DAY OF SECOND MANASSAS

In the summer of 1862, the Confederate fighting spirit was low. Faced with over-whelming casualties at the Battle of Shiloh and frequent Union raids into northern Virginia, the Confederacy needed a victory. They found one at the Battle of Second Bull Run (Second Manassas). Union troops were closing in on Confederate forces led by Robert E. Lee and "Stonewall" Jackson. They faced a surprise attack on their left flank from twenty-eight thousand Confederate troops led by General James Longstreet. The Union troops were forced to retreat, and—just as in first Manassas—their attack on northern Virginia was stalled. Leading Confederate cavalry forces in the battle was James Ewell Brown ("Jeb") Stuart, who also played a major role in the Confederate victory at the first Battle of Manassas. Stuart was one of the first Confederate generals to leave the Union. He had mailed the Confederacy's president, Jefferson Davis, a letter on January 1861 to ask for a place in the "Army of the South." He was made a general by the end of the year and gained a reputation as a brilliant military mind and a legendary reconnais-sance, or scouting, officer. In this battle report, Stuart describes the final afternoon of the Second Bull Run.

- **J.E.B. Stuart, Report on the Battle of Second Manassas, in *The War of the Rebellion*, series I, 53 volumes. Washington: Government Printing Office, 1880–1901.**

> **📓 GLOSSARY**
>
> - **enfilade:** attack with a line of gunfire
> - **cavalier:** cavalry soldier
> - **the Lord of Hosts:** God
> - **intelligence:** scouting reports
> - **resolute:** determined
> - **ignominious:** humiliating

A bout 3 p.m., the enemy having disclosed his movement on [Confederate General "Stonewall"] Jackson, our right wing advanced to the attack. I directed [Frank] Robertson's brigade and [Thomas] Rosser's regiment to push forward on the extreme right, and at the same time all the batteries I could get hold of were advanced at a gallop to take position to enfilade the enemy in front of our lines. This was done with splendid effect, Colonel Rosser, a fine artillerist, as well as bold cavalier, having the immediate direction of the batteries. The enemy's lines were distinctly visible and every shot told upon them fearfully. Robertson's brigade was late coming forward, and consequently our right flank was at one time somewhat threatened by the enemy's cavalry, but the artillery of Captain Rogers with a few well-directed shots relieved us on that score. When our cavalry

This print gives a panoramic view of the battlefield in the second Battle of Manassas. Union troops (foreground) were forced to flee after a surprise flank attack by the South turned the tide of the battle.

arrived on the field no time was lost in crowding the enemy, the artillery being kept always far in advance of the infantry lines. The fight was of remarkably short duration. The Lord of Hosts was plainly fighting on our side, and the solid walls of Federal infantry melted away before the straggling, but nevertheless determined, onsets of our infantry columns. The head of Robertson's cavalry was now on the ridge overlooking Bull Run, and having seen no enemy in that direction, I was returning to the position of the artillery enfilading the Groveton road, when I received intelligence from General Robertson at the point I had just left that the enemy was there in force and asking re-enforcements. I ordered the two reserve regiments (Seventh and Twelfth) rapidly forward, and also a section of artillery, but before the latter could reach the point our cavalry, by resolute bravery, had put the enemy, under [Union General John] Buford, to ignominious flight across Bull Run, and were in full pursuit until our own artillery fire at the fugitives rendered it dangerous to proceed farther.

★ Robert E. Lee ★

LEE'S LETTER TO THE PEOPLE OF MARYLAND

When the Confederacy formed in February 1861, Robert E. Lee was regarded as the Union's most competent officer. The Union lost Lee to the Confederacy when Virginia seceded in April 1861. Although he opposed slavery, Lee was more loyal to his home state than he was to the Union. Lee was building up defenses in South Carolina in March 1862 when Confederate president Jefferson Davis gave him a new assignment. He was to help defend Richmond, Virginia (the Confederate capital). Richmond was under attack by the Union's massive Army of the Potomac. Lee took command and successfully drove the Army of the Potomac away from Virginia. With the Union on the run, Lee decided to take on a more offensive strategy and lead the Confederacy's massive Army of Northern Virginia into the state of Maryland in the fall of 1862. Maryland was considered a "border state" during the Civil War, loyal to the Union but with legalized slavery and strong Confederate sympathies. President Abraham Lincoln took some strong and arguably unconstitutional measures to prevent the state from seceding, provoking great outrage in Maryland's citizenry. In this letter to the people of Maryland, Lee assures them that he means them no harm.

GLOSSARY

- **commonwealth:** state
- **allied:** connected
- **indignation:** resentment
- **pretense:** false appearance
- **venerable:** old
- **illustrious:** distinguished
- **usurped:** taken over
- **arbitrary:** unlawful
- **inalienable:** incapable of being transferred to others
- **sovereignty:** self-rule
- **despoiled:** robbed

- **Robert E. Lee, Address to the People of Maryland. September 8, 1862.**

To the People of Maryland: It is right that you should know the purpose that brought the army under my command within the limits of your State, so far as that purpose concerns yourselves. The people of the Confederate States have long watched with the deepest sympathy the wrongs and outrages that have been inflicted upon the citizens of a commonwealth allied to the States of the South by the strongest social, political, and commercial ties. They have seen with profound indignation their sister State deprived of every right and reduced to the condition of a conquered province. Under the pretense of supporting the Constitution, but in violation of its most valuable provisions, your citizens have been arrested and imprisoned upon no charge and contrary to all forms of law. The faithful and manly protest against this outrage made by the venerable and illustrious Marylander, to whom in better days no citizen appealed for right in vain, was

The Confederate cavalry fords the Potomac River and crosses into Maryland. Gen. Robert E. Lee led the invasion to liberate the state from Union control.

treated with scorn and contempt; the government of your chief city has been usurped by armed strangers; your legislature has been dissolved by the unlawful arrest of its members; freedom of the press and of speech has been suppressed; words have been declared offenses by an arbitrary decree of the Federal Executive, and citizens ordered to be tried by a military commission for what they may dare to speak. Believing that the people of Maryland possessed a spirit too lofty to submit to such a government, the people of the South have long wished to aid you in throwing off this foreign yoke, to enable you again to enjoy the inalienable rights of freemen, and restore independence and sovereignty to your State. In obedience to this wish, our army has come among you, and is prepared to assist you with the power of its arms in regaining the rights of which you have been despoiled.

This, citizens of Maryland, is our mission, so far as you are concerned. No constraint upon your free will is intended; no intimidation will be allowed within the limits of this army, at least. Marylanders shall once more enjoy their ancient freedom of thought and speech. We know no enemies among you, and will protect all, of every opinion. It is for you to decide your destiny freely and without constraint. This army will respect your choice, whatever it may be; and while the Southern people will rejoice to welcome you to your natural position among them, they will only welcome you when you come of your own free will.

★ *James Longstreet* ★

PICKETT'S CHARGE

General James Longstreet hailed from South Carolina, the first state to secede from the Union. He played a decisive role in several major Confederate victories and become known as one of the most skilled generals of the war. Longstreet served under General Robert E. Lee at the Battle of Gettysburg in July 1863. On the second day of fighting, Lee ordered soldiers under the command of Major-General George Pickett—a division that had never before served in combat—to charge uphill against heavily armed Union forces. More than 3,000 of the 4,500 soldiers in Pickett's division were killed. When the Battle of Gettysburg ended on July 3, 51,000 soldiers were dead, wounded, or missing. It was the bloodiest battle of the war, and a turning point in the struggle between the Confederacy and the Union. For months, Lee and his Army of Northern Virginia had defeated Union forces in a series of battles. This time, his army was in ruins and the Confederacy seemed close to defeat. In this excerpt from his official report, Longstreet describes the slaughter of Pickett's Charge.

- **James Longstreet, Report on the Gettysburg Campaign, in *The War of the Rebellion*, series I, 53 volumes. Washington: Government Printing Office, 1880–1901.**

The advance was made in very handsome style, all the troops keeping their lines accurately, and taking the fire of the batteries with great coolness and deliberation. About half way between our position and that of the enemy, a ravine partially sheltered our troops from the enemy's fire, where a short halt was made for rest. The advance was resumed after a moment's pause, all still in good order. The enemy's batteries soon opened upon our lines with canister, and the left seemed to stagger under it, but the advance was resumed, and with some degree of steadiness. Pickett's troops did not appear to be checked by the batteries, and only halted to deliver a fire when close under musket-range. . . . Pickett's troops, after delivering fire, advanced to the charge, and entered the enemy's lines. .

GLOSSARY

- **batteries:** cannons
- **canister:** artillery ammunition that was effective against infantry
- **checked:** halted
- **retiring:** retreating

. . About the same moment, the troops that had before hesitated, broke their ranks and fell back in great disorder, many more falling under the enemy's fire in retiring than while they were attacking. This gave the enemy time to throw his entire force upon Pickett, with a strong prospect of being able to break up his lines or destroy him. . . . He was, therefore, ordered to halt. In a few moments the enemy, marching against both flanks and the front of Pickett's division, overpowered it and drove it back, capturing about half of those of it who were not killed or wounded.

★ *Jubal Anderson Early* ★

FAILURE AT WASHINGTON, D.C.

A lawyer, politician, and retired soldier, Jubal A. Early opposed the secession of Virginia but chose to side with his home state when it left the Union in April 1861. He quickly rose up the Confederate ranks and served under Robert E. Lee in the Army of Northern Virginia. In 1864, Early was given his own command and a new assignment. He was to take control of the Union capital of Washington, D.C. If the Confederates seized Washington, they could win the war. In this excerpt from his report, Early describes the scene on July 11 and 12, as he prepared to march into Washington, D.C., and was forced to turn back.

- **Jubal A. Early, Report on Operations Against Washington, D.C. (July 14, 1864), in *The War of the Rebellion*, series I, 53 volumes. Washington: Government Printing Office, 1880–1901.**

O n the morning of the 11th we continued the march, but the day was so excessively hot, even at a very early hour in the morning, and the dust so dense, that many of the men fell by the way, and it became necessary to slacken our pace. Nevertheless, when we reached the right of the enemy's fortifications the men were almost completely exhausted and not in a condition to make an attack. . . . [Washington fortifications] we found to be very strong and constructed very scientifically. They consist of a circle of inclosed forts . . . and every approach swept by a cross-fire of artillery, including some heavy guns. I determined at first to make an assault, but before it could be made it became apparent that the enemy had been strongly re-enforced, and we knew that the Sixth Corps had arrived from Grant's army, and after consultation with my division commanders I became satisfied that the assault, even if successful, would be attended with such great sacrifice as would insure the destruction of my whole force before the victory could have been made available, and, if unsuccessful, would necessarily have resulted in the loss of the whole force. I, therefore, reluctantly determined to retire, and as it was evident preparations were making to cut off my retreat, and while troops were gathering around me I would find it difficult to get supplies. I determined to retire across the Potomac [River] to this county before it became too late. I was led to this determination by the conviction that the loss of my force would have had such a depressing effect upon the country, and would so encourage the enemy as to amount to a very serious, if not fatal, disaster to our cause. . . .

Washington can never be taken by our troops unless surprised when without a force to defend it.

> **GLOSSARY**
> - **conviction:** belief
> - **consultation:** meeting
> - **retire:** retreat

★ *John Brown Gordon* ★
HARD-EARNED RESPECT

John Brown Gordon

Georgia lawyer John Brown Gordon gained a reputation as a brilliant strategist and a popular leader. When the Civil War broke out, he was placed in command of the "Raccoon Roughs," a mountaineering force that made up a small part of the 6th Alabama Regiment. By the end of the war, he had become a full general. In this excerpt from his autobiography, Gordon describes the grudging respect that Union and Confederate soldiers showed each other by the war's end.

- **John B. Gordon, *Reminiscences of the Civil War.* New York: Scribner, 1903.**

I n 1861 a disorder had taken possession of the minds of the people in every section of the country. Internecine war, contagious, infectious, confluent, was spreading, and destined to continue spreading until nearly every home in the land was affected and hurt by it. This dreadful disease had about it some wonderful compensations. No one went through it from a high sense of duty without coming out of it a braver, a better, and a more consecrated man. It is a great mistake to suppose that war necessarily demoralizes and makes obdurate those who wage it. Doubtless wars of conquest, for the sake of conquest, for the purpose of despoiling the vanquished and enriching the victors, and all wars inaugurated from unhallowed motives, do demoralize every man engaged in them, from the commanding general to the privates. But such was not the character of our Civil War. On the contrary, it became a training-school for the development of an unselfish and exalted manhood, which increased in efficiency from its opening to its close. At the beginning there was personal antagonism and even bitterness felt by individual soldiers of the two armies toward each other. The very sight of the uniform of an opponent aroused some trace of anger. But this was all gone long before the conflict had ceased. It was supplanted by a brotherly sympathy.

★ John Bell Hood ★
UNFORTUNATE CIRCUMSTANCES

John Bell Hood was a native of Kentucky, but regarded Texas as his adoptive home. He joined the Confederacy when Texas seceded in April 1861. His string of victories throughout the early years of the Civil War earned him the rank of general. Troubled by Union general William T. Sherman's September 1864 victory in Atlanta and his attacks on civilian property in Georgia, Hood decided to attack Sherman's supply lines in Tennessee. He then hoped to reinforce Robert E. Lee's army in Virginia. Although Hood won some minor battles, the campaign was a costly failure. In this excerpt from his official report, Hood faults simple bad luck for his defeat. Despite this explanation, Hood was no longer confident in his ability to lead. He resigned from the Confederate army in January 1865.

John Bell Hood

- **John Bell Hood, Report on the Franklin-Nashville Campaign, in *The War of the Rebellion*, series I, 53 volumes. Washington: Government Printing Office, 1880–1901.**

My reasons for undertaking the movement into Tennessee have, I think, been sufficiently stated already. Had I not made the movement I am fully persuaded that [Union general William T.] Sherman would have been upon General Lee's communication in October, instead of at this time.

From Palmetto to Spring Hill the campaign was all that I could have desired. The fruits ought to have been gathered at that point. At Nashville, had it not have been for an unfortunate event which could not justly have been anticipated, I think we would have gained a complete victory. At any time it was in the power of the army to retire from Tennessee in the event of failure, as is established by the leisurely retreat which was made under the most difficult and embarrassing circumstances. It is my firm conviction that, not withstanding that disaster, I left the army in better spirits and with more confidence in itself than it had at the opening of the campaign. The official records will show that my losses, including prisoners, during the entire campaign do not exceed 10,000 men. Were I again placed in such circumstances I should make the same marches and fight the same battles, trusting that the same unforseen and unavoidable accident would not again occur to change into disaster a victory which had been already won.

GLOSSARY
- **communication:** line of communication
- **retire:** withdraw
- **leisurely:** slow
- **conviction:** belief

★ *Nathan Bedford Forrest* ★
SAVING MISSISSIPPI

In April 1864, Nathan Bedford Forrest's cavalry defeated Union troops at Fort Pillow, Tennessee. When the Union soldiers gave up the fort, Forrest's cavalry stormed it and slaughtered hundreds of Union soldiers, especially targeting African American troops. In June 1864, Forrest destroyed crucial Union supply lines at the Battle of Brice's Cross Roads in Mississippi. Soon after, at the Battle of Tupelo, Union troops led by General A.J. Smith attempted to attack Forrest's cavalry and prevent them from making similar raids in the future. As this excerpt from his report on the fighting near Tupelo makes clear, Forrest believed that the Union troops were the raiders. Forrest saw himself as a savior who defended Mississippi residents from Union troops.

- **Nathan B. Forrest, Report on the Battle of Harrisburg, in *The War of the Rebellion*, series I, 53 volumes. Washington: Government Printing Office, 1880–1901.**

I ordered immediate construction of temporary fortifications, and in a short time the men along my entire line were protected behind strong works erected out of the rails, logs, and cottonbales. . . .

On the morning of the 15th, finding the enemy could not be driven from his fortifications, [Confederate] General [Abraham] Buford was ordered to move up the Verona road and attack his left flank. General Buford pushed forward his troops and drove the enemy back about one mile, where he was protected by his main line. But few men were killed or wounded in this engagement, but I found the road strewn with men fainting under the oppressive heat, hard labor, and want of water. . . . I immediately proceeded to Harrisburg with General Roddey's command and attacked the enemy's rear guard, which, after a short engagement with Colonel Warren's regiment, retired. I ordered General Buford to press forward in the direction of Tupelo and engage the enemy there, if he still occupied the place. On reaching Harrisburg Lieutenant-General [Robert E.] Lee ordered me to take command of the troops and to pursue the enemy. . . . Having learned General Lee's desires I started from Tupelo to join my command. . . . On arriving at Old Town Creek I found [Confederate] General James R. Chalmers and General Buford hotly engaged. The enemy had selected a strong position on the crest of a hill, but was driven to the creek bottom by Bell's and Crossland's brigades, where he was heavily re-enforced, which enabled him not only to hold his posi-

GLOSSARY

- **commenced:** began
- **execution:** carrying out a plan
- **oppressive:** heavy
- **retired:** retreated
- **incapacitated:** disabled
- **spoliation:** looting, vandalism

This print depicts the slaughter of mostly African American Union troops by Gen. Nathan B. Forrest's Confederate soldiers. The Union soldiers had just surrendered Fort Pillow in Tennessee to Forrest.

tion, but to press back these two brigades. I ordered General Chalmers to move up with [Confederate general Henry] McCulloch's brigade, and [Confederate captain T.W.] Rice's battery to be placed in position, which for a time held the enemy in check. While riding across the field and endeavoring to press forward my left I received a painful wound, which incapacitated me from further service. . . .

The next morning the enemy renewed his retreat and was for two days [pursued]. . . . The enemy was thus driven back to the point from which he started and many a home saved from spoliation, and the country preserved from the desolation and ruin which everywhere marks the invader's tracks. But this achievement cost the best blood of the South.

★ *Robert E. Lee* ★
FAREWELL TO THE ARMY

This painting shows Confederate soldiers rolling up the Confederate flag after Robert E. Lee surrendered at Appomattox.

After he took command of the Confederacy's Army of Northern Virginia in June 1862, Robert E. Lee quickly showed the traits that led military historians to classify him as the greatest general of the war. Often facing overwhelming odds, Lee achieved battlefield victories through his bold strategies. Without enough reinforcements, however, Lee could not overpower the Union army. Eventually his own army shrank and was pursued by larger federal forces. Relentlessly attacked by Union general Ulysses S. Grant's Army of the Potomac, Lee and the Army of the Northern Virginia were cornered in April 1865 at Appomattox, Virginia. Facing certain defeat, with tens of thousands of likely casualties, Lee surrendered on April 9. In this official farewell to his army, Lee resigns his Confederate commission and essentially ends the four-year conflict that tore the nation apart.

• Robert E. Lee, Farewell to His Army, April 10, 1865.

Head-Quarters, Army of Northern Virginia, April 10, 1865.
After four years of arduous service, marked by unsurpassed courage and fortitude, the Army of Northern Virginia has been compelled to yield to overwhelming numbers and resources. I need not tell the survivors of so many hard-fought battles, who have remained steadfast to the last, that I have consented to this result from no distrust of them: but, feeling that valour and devotion could accomplish nothing that could compensate for the loss that would have attended the continuation of the contest, I have determined to avoid the useless sacrifice of those whose past services have endeared them to their countrymen. By the terms of the agreement, officers and men can return to their homes and remain there until exchanged. You will take with you the satisfaction that proceeds from the consciousness of duty faithfully performed; and I earnestly pray that a merciful God will extend to you His blessing and protection. With an increasing admiration of your constancy and devotion to your country, and a grateful remembrance of your kind and generous consideration of myself, I bid you an affectionate farewell.

GLOSSARY
- **arduous:** very difficult
- **fortitude:** strength
- **compelled:** forced
- **steadfast:** loyal
- **compensate:** make up for, repay

FOR FURTHER READING

Books

Christin Ditchfield. *Joseph E. Johnston*. Bloomall, PA: Chelsea House, 2001. This biography addresses Johnston's major role in the Civil War and his postwar life as a successful politician.

Carl Green and William R. Sanford. *Confederate Generals of the Civil War*. Berkeley Heights, NJ: Enslow, 1998. Provides short biographies of the best-known Confederate generals.

Meg Greene. *James Ewell Brown Stuart*. Bloomall, PA: Chelsea House, 2001. This biography focuses on Stuart's role as the Confederate "eyes of the army."

Chris Hughes. *Stonewall Jackson*. San Diego, CA: Blackbirch Press/Gale Group, 2001. This 104-page biography focuses on Jackson's important role during the early years of the Civil War, and the effect his death had on the South.

David C. King. *Robert E. Lee*. San Diego, CA: Blackbirch Press/Gale Group, 2001. This biography follows the same general format as the Jackson volume described above, placing emphasis on how Lee's actions affected, and were affected by, other personalities and events of the Civil War.

Melanie LeTourneau. *James Longstreet*. San Diego, CA: Blackbirch Press/Gale Group, 2002. Like the Jackson and Lee volumes described above, this Triangle Histories biography of Longstreet examines his role as a military commander and addresses how his actions influenced, and were influenced by, other major figures of the Civil War.

Websites

The American Civil War Home Page
http://sunsite.utk.edu/civil-war The largest online directory of Civil War resources, maintained by Dr. George H. Hoemann of the University of Tennessee. Includes biographical information on Confederate generals.

The Civil War Home Page
http://www.civil-war.net A database of Civil War history, with detailed information on specific battles and campaigns.

INDEX